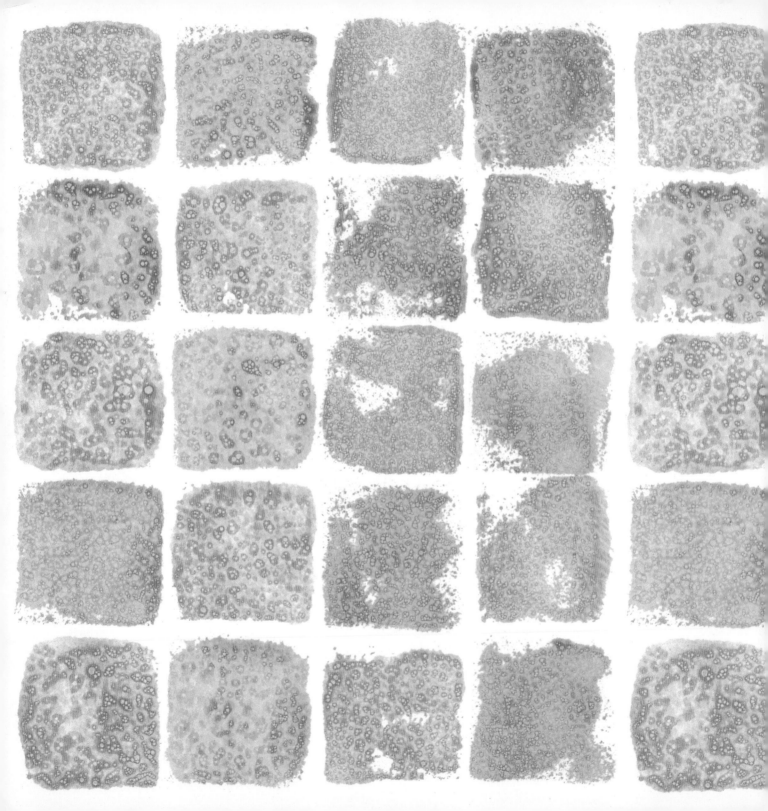

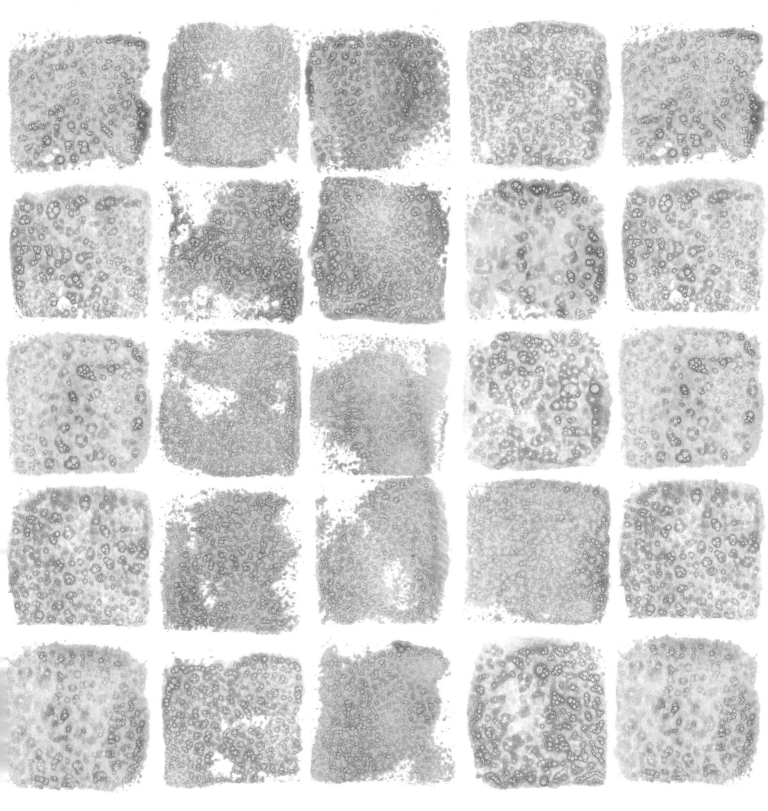

Ceramic and Glassware Style

Ceramic and Glassware Style

**PAINT YOUR OWN
TABLEWARE, GLASSWARE, AND
DECORATIVE OBJECTS**

Alma Caira

Watson-Guptill Publications/New York

First published in the United States in 2000
by Watson-Guptill Publications,
a division of BPI Communications, Inc.,
770 Broadway, New York, N.Y. 10003

Library of Congress Catalog Card Number: 00–102710

ISBN 0-8230-0588-7

Conceived and produced by Breslich & Foss Ltd., London

Set in Bodoni and Gill Sans

Printed and bound in Spain by Bookprint, S. L.,Barcelona.

First printing, 2000

1 2 3 4 5 6 7 8 9 / 08 07 06 05 04 03 02 01 00

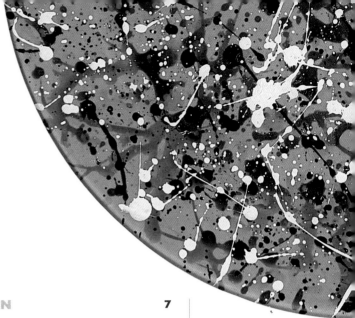

CONTENTS

INTRODUCTION

People have been decorating china and glass for many centuries, and one of the most popular methods has been the simple application of paint. While this technique may at first seem limited, variations in color, form, and texture create an infinite range of possibilities. China and glass share many of the same properties, and all the techniques in this book can be used on either surface, but with surprisingly different results, thanks to the transparent nature of glass.

This book aims to equip you with a range of techniques, and plenty of inspiration. There are templates at the back of the book, and I hope that after trying a few of the projects you will feel confident enough to produce your own designs.

If you find the prospect of applying color to a plain surface daunting, just remember that if you make a mistake you can always wash the paint off and start again. Choose colors that you love as a basis for your designs, and you can't go far wrong. You may make a few "mistakes" along the way, but sometimes the best designs are created this way.

One of the benefits of producing your own designs is that you can tailor them to your own preferences, reflecting your interests and tastes, and matching your color schemes exactly. China- and glass-painting is also an invaluable means of producing unique presents for friends, though you may find that the biggest problem you have is parting with your much-loved creations.

There is an abundance of plain, beautifully shaped china and glassware available, and I hope that by leafing through this book you will find plenty of ideas for transforming that forgotten plate or vase that's been stored away for ages, allowing it once again to take pride of place in your home.

Painting on china and glass is good fun. I really hope you enjoy recreating the following projects, or adapting them to create your own designs. So gather your paints together, put your apron on, roll up your sleeves, and give it a try!

Materials and Techniques

Paints

There is a huge range of paint products for ceramic- and glass-painting on the market. Many paints are suitable for both surfaces, but do read the manufacturer's literature before making your choice. This choice will largely depend on whether the object to be painted is to be functional or purely decorative. For example, oil- (solvent-) based paints and the so-called "cold" water-based ceramic paints are unsuitable for objects intended for use with food.

Water-Based Paint

Water-based ceramic paints that do not need baking are pleasant to use, and mistakes can easily be wiped off with a paper towel or cotton swab (cotton bud) dipped in water. These are the best paints for children to use, as they are non-toxic and brushes can be washed out in water. The colors can be mixed, but you have to work relatively quickly because the paint dries fast. You can apply successive coats, but be careful not to disturb the paint underneath. These "cold" ceramic paints are great for decorative objects, but are unsuitable for surfaces that come into regular contact with food as the paint may scratch off.

The best paint to use for kitchenware is water-based paint that requires baking in a domestic oven. Thermo-hardening fixes the colors and results in a tough finish that can withstand dishwashing. The colors remain true provided that you follow the guidelines for the baking times and temperature. It is vital to let the finished piece dry for at least 24 hours before baking. If the paint is not dry before baking, air bubbles may appear on the surface.

Heat-set paints were previously restricted to ceramics, but there is a new line on the market from Pébéo that has opened up this possibility for glass, too. Thermo-hardening glass paint is similar in appearance to ceramic paint, but applying successive coats is trickier, as previous coats have a tendency to lift off unless you are gentle.

When buying china and glass for kitchen use you must be absolutely certain that it will withstand the temperature that is required to harden the paint. Also, check the label to see whether your item is dishwasher safe. Some products, such as recycled glass, are not suitable and should be hand-washed with care. The same rule applies to second-hand shop finds, as you cannot be certain of what you are buying.

Oil-Based Paints

Oil- (solvent-) based paints are suitable only for decorative pieces, and must never be used on objects that are likely to come into contact with the mouth. Oil-based paints have a longer drying time, which means that the paint has more time to spread evenly, therefore making brush marks less visible. This quality means that the paint tends to slide down the sides of curved surfaces. You can take advantage of this by creating interesting marbling effects as different colors spread into each other. The paint is generally more transparent than water-based paint, and it can be diluted with mineral spirits (white spirit) to improve the flow even further. Brushes must be washed out right away in mineral spirits (white spirit). Always work in a well-ventilated room when using these paints, which are not thermo-hardening.

Opposite Clockwise from the top: paintbrushes, masking fluid, porcelain and glass pens, etching tools, craft knife, assorted ceramic and glass paints, outliner pastes, gels, and sponges.

Right Outliner pastes are useful for creating simple drawings on glass and ceramic bases.

Outliner Pastes

Outliner pastes come in a wide range of colors, and create a raised line that can be used as a neat border for around areas of glass or ceramic paint, or to draw linear patterns. Some pastes require oven baking, and are compatible with the water-based thermo-hardening glass and ceramic paints. For purely decorative use, there are metallic pastes that do not require baking. A stained-glass effect can be achieved using black outliner in combination with colored gels. (For gels, see next column.)

Porcelain and Glass Pens

These special pens come in a range of colors, finishes, and thicknesses. They are thermo-hardening and are useful for creating quick line drawings on ceramics and glassware. The wider-tipped pens are useful for filling in large areas, while you can achieve a great deal of detail with the finer ones.

Gel

This is a water-based product for glass that comes in a tube. It can be used to draw raised lines, and you can buy attachment nozzles to squeeze out thicker or thinner lines. Used straight from the tube, gel can be modelled with a knife to create a relief effect. When it is shaken or stirred, however, it becomes liquid and can be applied with a brush. The method of application greatly affects the drying time. When working with gel, bear in mind that it will shrink slightly when it dries. This is a good product to use on a curved object, as the gel stays malleable but will not drip.

Gels are available in transparent, opalescent, and glitter finishes and can be baked in the oven to improve their water resistance.

Varnishes and Mediums

If you have chosen to use cold ceramic paint, you might like to protect your work by applying a coat of clear varnish. Gloss, matte, or tinted varnish will alter the appearance of the design.

Mediums come in a wider range of effects, such as frosted and opalescent finishes and crackle glazing. Mediums can be combined with the paint before application, or applied over the dried item. They do not afford much protection, however, and should be used in conjunction with a varnish that you have applied after baking the piece in the usual way.

Thinners alter the flow of the paint without affecting its color or adhesion and are useful for creating a wash of paint over a large area.

The arrival of "pottery cafes" has created an opportunity to experiment with professional glazes that require firing in a kiln at high temperatures. The way these cafes are usually run is that you pay for each object that you wish to paint, then there is a small fee for the glazes you use and for the kiln time. This is a really enjoyable way to paint ceramics in a relaxed environment with some friendly help at hand, and tea and cake on tap!

EQUIPMENT

Here are the basic items that you will need for the projects in this book:

Sketchbook

For planning your own designs and testing color variations. Use a variety of paints such as gouache and watercolors to practice your brush skills. This is where you should keep all your ideas for future projects.

Permanent Marker Pens

Used to draw designs on to china and glass.

Old China, Tiles, and Glass

Painting on glass and ceramic requires a little practice. Doing tests also allows you to see how the paints will look on the intended surface. White tiles are inexpensive and easy to come by, and can be baked in the oven so that you can see exactly how the colors will blend together.

Tracing Paper

For creating repeat patterns and reverse stencils.

Masking Tape

For securing stencils and transfer (carbon) paper to objects. Masking tape can be used to create patterns.

Stencil Board and Acetate

Stencil board is useful for creating long-lasting stencils. Acetate is also used for stencils, and as a material on which to test glass paint.

Masking Film

For creating a mask on flat and cylindrical objects.

Transfer (Carbon) Paper

For transferring designs to objects.

China Markers

For drawing guidelines on china and glass.

Craft Knife and Scissors

Used extensively to cut out stencils, etch patterns in paint, etc.

Sponges

Closely textured sponges can be cut into simple shapes and made into stamps. Use a decorator's sponge or a pan scourer for this purpose. A natural sea sponge has a much more open surface, and is ideal for creating texture.

Palette or Saucer

For mixing paint and wiping off brushes and sponges if you need a dry finish.

Craft Foam

Useful for creating malleable shapes for stamping on glass and china.

Linoleum and Cutting Tools

Linoleum makes really sturdy stamps. Linoleum cutting tools are used to gouge linear patterns into the linoleum. The blades are sharp, so always direct tools away from you.

Cutting Mat and Steel Ruler

For cutting out stencils. The ruler is also useful for guiding pens across a surface.

Paper Towel

For blotting sponges and wiping off excess paint. Can also be used to apply paint.

Cotton Swabs (Buds)

For wiping away mistakes and etching into wet paint.

Paintbrushes

- Fine, pointed brushes for painting outlines and fine detail.
- Medium, pointed brushes for general work.
- Large, pointed brushes for filling in larger areas.
- Chisel-shaped brushes for drawing wide, straight lines.
- Stipple brushes for stenciling or creating a texture similar to sponging.

Assortment packs are available in art supply and craft stores, however it makes sense to buy the best brushes that you can afford. They will reward you by lasting longer than cheap ones if you treat them well. Avoid using synthetic brushes as the bristles tend to fall out and the brushmarks are more visible. Natural-hair brushes are the best option and can be used for both water- and oil- (solvent-) based paints, provided that you clean them thoroughly after each use and shape the hairs back into a point.

TECHNIQUES

Prepare ceramic and glass objects for painting by gently washing them in warm, soapy water to remove any greasy marks or labels. Allow them to dry thoroughly before painting.

Measuring the Circumference of a Plate

Run a strip of masking tape around the outside edge of the plate, then cut the tape exactly to size. Remove the masking tape, lay it on a flat surface, then measure it with a ruler. This will give you the circumference of the plate. Divide this measurement into equal amounts in order to create a uniform pattern. Wrap the tape around the plate again, and mark the plate at the points that you have indicated on the tape.

Locating the Center of a Plate

Take a ruler and slide it over the plate until you find the widest point. Mark the center point of that measurement and draw a line through it with a water-soluble pen or china marker. Repeat this at least twice at different points. The lines will cross each other and will define the center point. Alternatively, follow the instructions for measuring the circumference of the plate. Once you have cut the tape to the correct length, mark the halfway point, reapply the tape and then draw a line between the halfway point and where the edges of the tape meet. Repeat this process at least once more. The center point is at the junction where the lines cross. Once you know how to find the center of a plate and how to divide the circumference, you will be able to create any measured design.

Measuring Cylindrical Objects

The masking tape technique works for these objects, too. Wrap the strip of masking tape around your object and cut it to fit exactly. Remove it and measure the length of it as before. Divide the measurement into equal amounts to create your chosen pattern. (Remember to take handles into account when planning the design.)

Sponging

Sponging is an effective way to cover a surface quickly and evenly. A layer of sponged paint is also a subtle base for the next stage of a design, such as a freehand drawing. Sponges can be cut into simple shapes, such as hearts or stars. This technique produces a slightly ragged edge, as the paint will inevitably seep away from the sponge. There are several different types of sponge available, and they all create different textures. Natural sea sponge has a much more open texture than a decorator's sponge or a pan scourer. Closely textured sponges are better for cutting out shapes. Experiment with using the sponge dry or slightly damp.

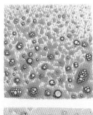

Stenciling

Stenciling produces a very precise edge that is useful if you are trying to create a repeat pattern. Keep the brush quite dry when stenciling, so that paint doesn't seep under the stencil. Stencil board, which is available from craft stores, is very durable. Acetate is another reusable material, but it is prone to tearing. As acetate is transparent, it allows you to place the stencil in a precise place and line up the design exactly. However, they are both unsuitable for stenciling curved surfaces because they are such inflexible materials. To stencil round or cylindrical objects, cut the stencil out of wide masking tape or self-adhesive film. If the design you wish to reproduce is small you may be able to use stencil board or acetate with double-sided tape behind it to lend additional support.

Stamping

Linoleum is the best stamping material to use for flat surfaces, and craft foam for curved surfaces. The best way to apply paint to a stamp is with a brush. This allows you to control how much paint goes on the stamp, and you can introduce more than one color at a time.

Above Simple stamped shapes can be enhanced with lines and dots of outliner paste.

Below These strawberries were created by adding yellow details to the sponged fruit. The stalks were then painted on in green.

Masking with Fluid

When applied to your chosen object, masking fluid acts as a resist. Paint applied over it will adhere only to the areas around it. It is best applied to a dry surface with a brush, and must be allowed to dry thoroughly before you paint over the top. This technique works best with a thin layer of paint, as the resist becomes harder to remove when there is a heavy coating over it. Once dry, it should be peeled or rubbed off with a finger. It is a good idea to draw the design with a china marker before applying the masking fluid; the lines will be removed with the fluid. Be stringent about cleaning brushes with soapy water as soon as you have used masking fluid, or they will be ruined.

Painting Freehand

This is perhaps the most exciting way to create a design, as any imperfections will simply enhance the handmade quality of the piece. With a stencil or a stamp you are confined to a repeat pattern that is always the same size and shape, but when drawing by hand you can adapt the design as you please. If you are nervous about using a paintbrush, begin with ceramic and glass pens, as they are much easier to control. A paintbrush gives a much nicer contrast in the thickness of the line, however, and brushmarks will add even more charm to the piece.

Masking with Tape

Masking tape used from the roll is a good material for creating regular designs, such as gingham or tartan, which require straight lines. Applying torn masking tape makes a nice random edge that you couldn't achieve by hand, and which is especially effective around a border. Pinking shears produce a serrated edge that is different from the torn masking tape. This technique requires little or no tidying up afterwards because the tape allows barely any paint to seep under it.

Above Masking tape can be used straight from the roll, or torn to give it an interesting edge.
Right These swirls were created with a combination of china marker and masking fluid.

Etching

Designs can be etched out of wet and dry paint with very different results. Etching tools for wet paint have shaped tips made from a rubbery material, and are very flexible. Use them to draw simple, bold lines, keeping a paper towel handy to wipe excess paint from the tip of the tool. Etching out of wet paint gives a softer line than from dry paint, which results in a more ragged edge. Dry paint must be scratched from the surface of the painted item with a sharp object, such as a craft knife, toothpick, or dried-up ballpoint pen.

Gilding

There are different methods of applying metal leaf, so it is important to read the manufacturer's instructions carefully before you begin. Gold and silver leaf can be left "bare," or painted over with glass paint. It's a good idea to varnish the leaf if you don't paint over it, as it will tarnish otherwise.

Creating Your Own Designs

Keep a scrapbook of patterns and colors that catch your eye, such as pictures in magazines, postcards, swatches of fabric, and gift wrap. You can adapt a design by simplifying it or changing its shape to fit your object. A complicated design can be simplified by tracing over it and leaving out the more complex features. You can change the size of a design by enlarging or reducing it on a photocopier, or by making a repeat pattern of one area. Changing the color of a pattern can alter it quite radically.

Using the Templates

The templates at the back of this book are intended to be used as inspiration for your own designs. The easiest way to adjust their size to fit the object you intend to decorate is by enlarging or reducing them on a photocopier. First, decide whether your design will be a repeat pattern or a single image, then measure the area you wish to cover (see page 12). Once you have your photocopies, transfer the design to your ceramic or glass object following the guidelines given below. (If the template you require happens to fit your object perfectly, trace it directly from the book with tracing paper.)

Transferring a Design

The best way to transfer a design to a transparent object is to trace the design through the glass with a china marker. Permanent pens can be used when you wish to follow the drawn lines, as they will show through the paint. Where the inside of a transparent object is inaccessible, or when working on ceramic, transfer the design with transfer (carbon) paper. Trace the template on to a sheet of tracing paper. Lay the tracing paper over a piece of transfer (carbon) paper cut to the same size, then draw over the lines in pencil to transfer the markings to your object. If the design you wish to transfer is a simple outline, a star for example, cut around the shape then draw around it.

If a project calls for masking film, simply lay this over the template and trace the outline onto the backing paper.

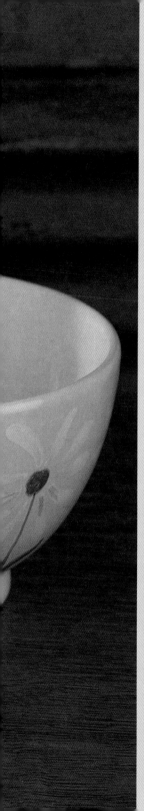

Painting Ceramics

HANDPAINTED CERAMICS HAVE A PARTICULAR CHARM ALL OF THEIR OWN.

THE FOLLOWING PROJECTS DEMONSTRATE HOW A RANGE OF QUICK AND EASY

TECHNIQUES CAN BE USED TO DECORATE BOTH WHITE AND COLORED PIECES.

MATERIALS

Yellow ceramic jug
Medium paintbrush

White, green, and, orange ceramic paint
Yellow ceramic outliner paste

Daisy Jug

Daisies are among the easiest

flowers to paint, and look

charming on a colored

background such as this creamy

yellow jug. Why not decorate

other pieces to match? A chain of

single daisies would look very

pretty painted around the

border of a plate, for example.

1 To create the petals of each daisy, apply single strokes of white paint, working from the center of the flower outward. Allow to dry.

2 Rinse the brush, then paint the stems and leaves with the green paint. Allow to dry.

3 Add tiny dots of yellow outliner paste to the center of each flower, then allow to dry.

4 Add darker touches to the centers with dots of orange ceramic paint. When dry, bake in the oven following the manufacturer's instructions.

Pet's Water Dish

Make the animals in your life feel appreciated by giving them their own handpainted bowls. To decorate the inside of the bowl, you can use the dog or cat designs at the back of the book, or paint your pet freehand. Trim the sides of the bowl by tracing the bone motifs from the finished projects on pages 22 and 23, or use the paw print template on page 132. These dishes are intended to hold water rather than pet food, as they will endure less punishment that way!

MATERIALS

White ceramic food or water dish
Templates from pages 22, 23, and 132
Masking film
Cutting mat
Craft knife
Sponge
Medium and fine paintbrushes

Red, white, black, and brown
   ceramic paint

The instructions given on pages 22–23 are for the dog design, but there is no need for the family cat to feel left out! Make a dish for a cat using the same method, with blue, orange, and black ceramic paint.

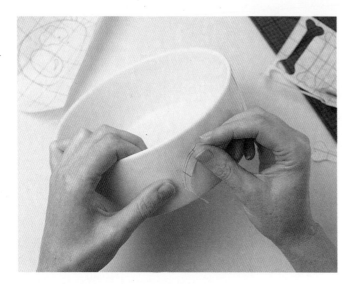

1 Photocopy the dog and bone templates to fit the size of your dish. Lay the masking film over the copies and trace over the shapes with a pencil. Cut these out with a craft knife and stick them firmly to the dish. It is a good idea to cut out the dog's features at this stage, as the shapes will help you follow the lines when you paint the face in step 4.

2 Sponge the dish inside and out with the background color, then let dry thoroughly. If the dish needs several coats of paint for even coverage, let each one dry before applying the next. Allow the final coat to dry before proceeding to step 3.

3 Carefully run the tip of the craft knife under the edges of the masking film, then gently lift a corner of the film with the blade before peeling it off. The film should lift off cleanly.

4 Paint the markings with white, black, and brown paint, using the shapes that were created by cutting out the features as guides. Paint a black line around the face and bones with the fine paintbrush. Add finishing touches by painting white highlights on the nose and right eye. When dry, bake in the oven following the manufacturer's instructions.

Chilies Olive Oil Bottle

This Mexican-style design would be perfect for a whole set of tableware. The chilies are printed with foam stamps that are suitable for use on both flat and curved surfaces. An oversized serving dish or salad bowl would look fantastic painted with a mass of chilies of different sizes and colors. Or you might like to design stamps for other fruits and vegetables. (Printed fabric is a good source for design ideas.)

MATERIALS

White ceramic olive oil bottle
Sponge
Pen
Craft knife
Cutting mat
Craft foam
Paintbrushes

Yellow, green, and red ceramic paint

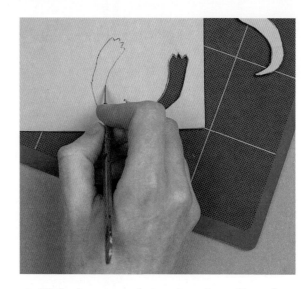

2 While the paint is drying, draw the outlines of two chili peppers on a piece of craft foam. Cut the shapes out of the foam with a craft knife.

1 Sponge yellow ceramic paint over the entire bottle.

3 Use a brush to apply a little green paint to one of the stamps, then press it against the surface of the bottle. Repeat as necessary, then allow to dry. (Handling stamps this size is a little tricky, but the results are worth the effort.)

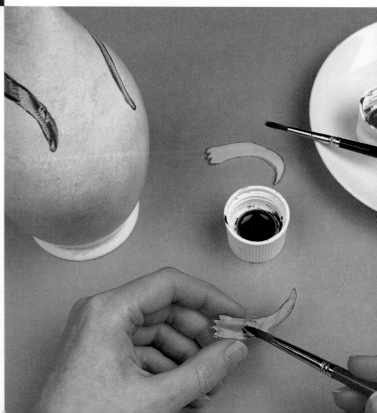

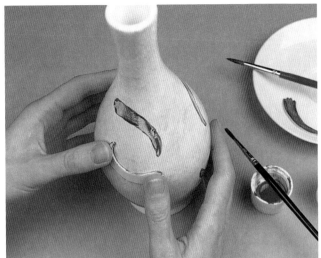

4 Apply red paint to the second stamp with a clean paintbrush, then stamp the bottle in one of the spaces between the green chilies. Repeat until the bottle is covered with red and green chili shapes. Allow to dry.

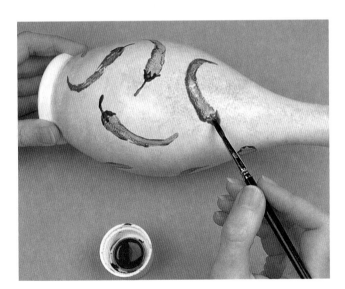

5 Paint a green stalk at the top of each chili. When dry, bake in the oven following the manufacturer's instructions.

Polka Dot Bowl

This fun design is created by using petroleum jelly to mask off the areas you don't want to paint. It is a great project for children to try, but be sure to protect work surfaces with plenty of paper before they begin. The technique can be used on a range of objects including teapots and mugs, and to create all kinds of random patterns, such as the stripes shown on the opposite page.

MATERIALS

White ceramic bowl
Petroleum jelly
Large paintbrush
Stipple brush or old toothbrush
Paper towels

Red, blue, yellow, green, and
  white ceramic paint

1 Draw the outlines of circles on the bowl using your fingertip and the petroleum jelly. Apply the petroleum jelly heavily between the circles so that the paint won't stick there.

2 Apply the first colors to the bowl with a large paintbrush, making sure that they are evenly spaced. The paint should be applied thickly so that it does not dry too quickly.

3 Apply the remaining colors. Allow the paint to run into the other colors in places to create a random, dribbled effect.

While the paint is still wet, use a hard stipple brush or an old toothbrush to spatter the entire bowl with each of the four colors. Finish off by spattering some white ceramic paint over the other colors. Because the spattering is done when the paint is still wet, all the colors will merge slightly.

5 When the paint is completely dry, gently remove the petroleum jelly with a paper towel, then wash the bowl in warm, soapy water. When dry, bake in the oven following the manufacturer's instructions.

Zebra Vase

Strips of masking tape are applied in V and Y shapes to create the zebra markings in this striking vase. For the best result, choose a tall, straight-sided vessel or one with a very slight curve. The technique can also be applied to plates to make an unusual dinner set.

MATERIALS

White, straight-sided ceramic vase
Masking tape
Stipple brush

Brown and black ceramic paint

1 Apply strips of torn masking tape to your vase using the photograph on the opposite page as a guide to position.

2 Stipple black paint from the top edge of the first stripe to about halfway down the vase.

3 While the paint is still wet, clean the brush, then use it to apply the brown paint, working from the base of the vase toward the top.

The technique used on the Zebra Vase can also be applied to flat objects, such as dining plates and serving dishes. In the example shown here (right), ragged strips of masking tape were laid in parallel bands.

4 Merge the two colors together where they meet. Work on one section at a time so that the paint doesn't dry too quickly and remains manageable. Apply additional coats until you are happy with the depth of color, letting each coat dry before applying the next.

5 When the last coat of paint is dry, carefully peel off the masking tape. Bake the vase in the oven following the manufacturer's instructions.

Turtle Serving Dish

The oval dish that I have used for this project complements the outline of the turtle perfectly, but the design would work just as well on a round plate. The method of stenciling gives a very crisp finish to the lines and contrasts well with the etched border. If you would prefer to repeat the turtle design around the edge of the dish, you may. First reduce the pattern on a photocopier and make lots of copies. Attach these to the rim following the method given in step 7. Then scratch out the design with a craft knife, by following the transfer lines.

MATERIALS

White ceramic serving dish
Templates from pages 41 and 133
Masking film
Masking tape
Scissors
Cutting mat
Craft knife

Sponge
Transfer (carbon) paper
Tracing paper
Pencil

Black and terracotta
    ceramic paint

1 Photocopy the turtle template to fit the size of your plate. Lay a sheet of masking film over the template, then trace the turtle on the film.

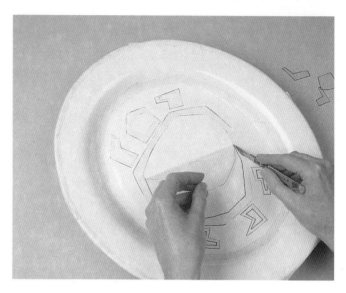

2 Apply strips of torn masking tape to the inner and outer edges of the rim. Cut out the turtle shapes, then position them on the plate, using the template as a guide. Press down on the pieces so that they adhere to the plate firmly.

3 Cut around the inside line of the turtle body with a craft knife and remove the center. (Keep the backing paper from the body of the turtle to use in step 7.) Repeat for the head and limbs.

4 Sponge black paint over the turtle and the rim. Let the first coat dry, then repeat until the surface is evenly covered, allowing each coat to dry before applying the next.

5 Clean the sponge, then use it to apply terracotta paint to the remainder of the plate. Repeat until the surface is evenly covered, letting each coat dry before applying the next.

6 When the paint is completely dry, peel off the masking tape. Run the tip of the craft knife under the edges of the masking film shapes, then carefully remove them.

7 Cut out the turtle's body shape in transfer (carbon) paper using the leftover backing paper from step 3 as the pattern. Lay the paper over the painted body, treated side down. Trace the shell markings from the template to a sheet of tracing paper. Lay the tracing paper over the transfer (carbon) paper, then draw over the lines in pencil to transfer the markings to the plate.

8 Scratch over the faint transfer (carbon) lines made in step 7 with a craft knife so that the surface of the plate shows through.

9 Add details to the head using the same technique, then scratch lines around the border. Bake in the oven following the manufacturer's instructions.

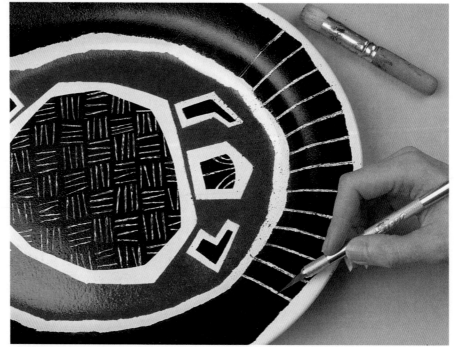

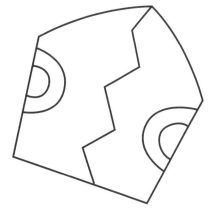

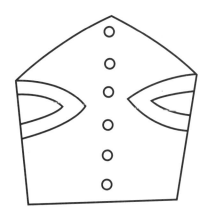

Keep your design for the turtle's features bold and simple. Here (left) are three templates for you to choose from.

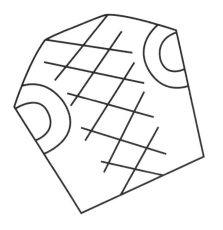

1950s Plate

The colors chosen for this project are very reminiscent of those found in 1950s design, especially when combined with a square plate as they are here. You could use a round plate so long as it has a very shallow rim. The templates work best on flat surfaces because they are cut from stencil board, which is a rigid material. If you wanted to decorate cups and bowls to match a set of these plates, simply repeat the outliner design from step 5 on the curved surfaces.

MATERIALS

Square white ceramic plate
Templates from pages 134 and 135
Tracing paper
Pencils (soft and hard)
Stencil board
Masking tape
Cutting mat
Craft knife
Double-sided tape
Scissors
Stipple brush

Red and blue ceramic paint
Black and gold ceramic outliner paste

1 Trace the first template on tracing paper with a soft pencil. Place the tracing pencil side down over the stencil board, and secure it with masking tape. Draw over the lines with a hard pencil to transfer the design. Remove the tracing paper and you will see the design on the stencil board. Cut out the design with a craft knife. Repeat with the second stencil.

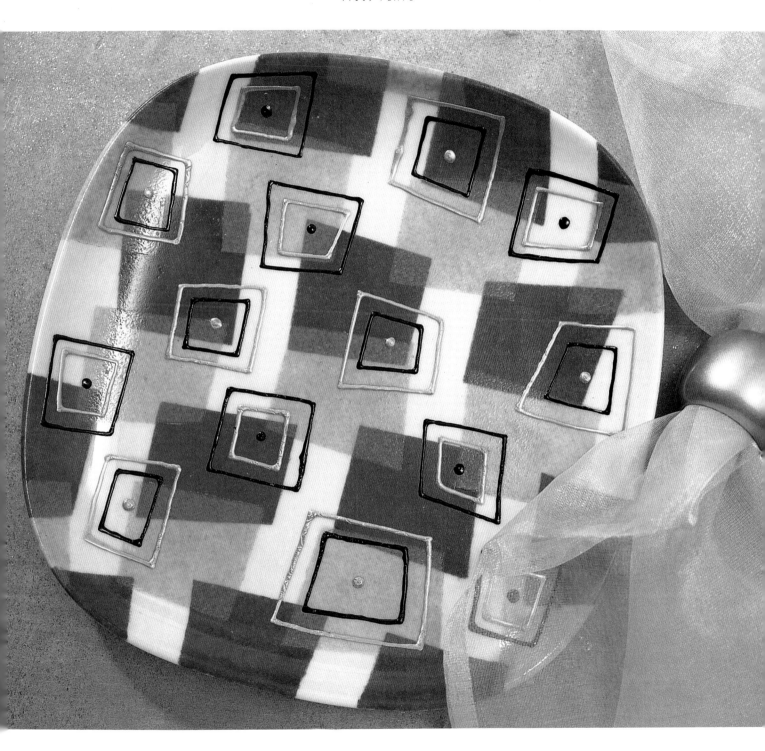

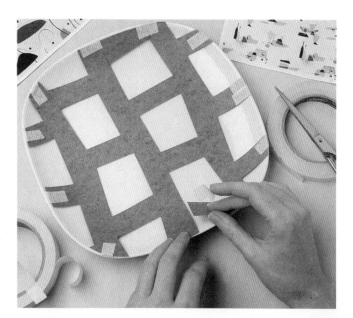

2 Attach the first stencil to the plate by applying double-sided tape to the center of the design. Snip the edges of the stencil with scissors and apply masking tape to the cuts to keep the stencil flat. This method will work on a round plate, too.

3 When the stencil is lying flat against the plate, stipple on the red ceramic paint. Apply successive coats until the plate is evenly covered, allowing the paint to dry between applications.

4 When the paint is dry, carefully remove the first stencil and apply the second stencil following the method given above in step 2. Use a clean stipple brush to apply several coats of blue paint, letting each coat dry before applying the next. Allow to dry, then remove the stencil.

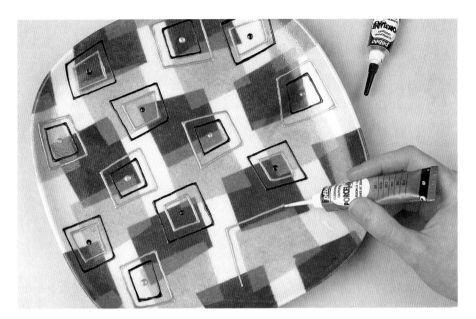

5 Draw black and gold lines with the outliner paste to link the rectangles created by the stencils. To begin, draw large, slightly off-kilter squares that overlap the stenciled shapes, alternating pen colors as you work.

6 Make a smaller, similar shape inside each box with the second color and finish it off with a dot of the first color in the center. Work your way around the plate with alternating colors. Allow to dry completely and bake in the oven following the manufacturer's instructions.

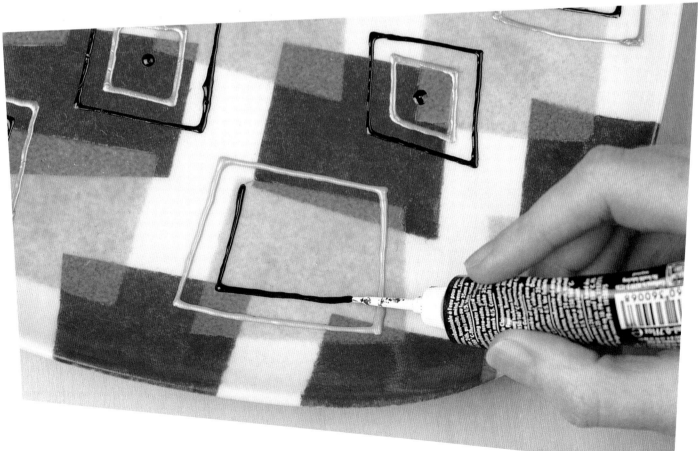

Stripy Plant Pot

Wet-etching is a very simple way to achieve a sophisticated look on a variety of objects. Paint this design on a group of different-sized plant pots and line them up on a windowsill for an eye-catching display. You can also apply the design to the border of a saucer or tile for the pot to sit on.

MATERIALS

White ceramic plant pot
Scissors
Sponge
Pointed and chisel-shaped etching tools
Paper towels

Green and turquoise ceramic paint

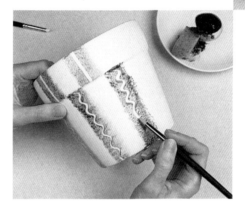

1 Cut a piece of sponge so that one end forms a square. Load the sponge with green paint, then use it to apply vertical bands from under the rim to the base, and around the rim. (Sponge one section at a time.)

2 While the paint is still wet, use the pointed etching tool to make a wavy line down the center of each band on the pot. Clean the tool on a paper towel as you work.

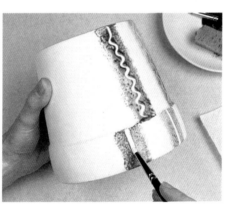

3 While the paint is still wet, draw a straight line into each band on the rim of the pot with the chisel-shaped tool. Continue sponging and etching alternating lines until you reach your starting point. Allow to dry.

4 Repeat steps 1 to 3 with the turquoise paint and a new piece of sponge. When dry, bake in the oven following the manufacturer's instructions.

"Jackson Pollock" Plate

This is another project with plenty of child appeal, one that youngsters can do on a table outdoors on a nice day. The technique is very simple, but the results are incredibly effective. For the paint to spatter correctly, its consistency should be very runny, so you will need to dilute it with ceramic paint thinner. Note that the effect of the spatter will vary, depending on the surface; when used on a rounded object, like a teapot, the paint will run and drip. Here, I have chosen a colored plate and limited the paint colors to four, but you may prefer to use a white plate and add more colors.

MATERIALS

Green ceramic plate
Paper cups
Ceramic paint thinner
Large paintbrushes

Green, blue, black, and white
   ceramic paint

1 Pour the ceramic paints that you intend to use into separate paper cups and add enough thinner to them to make the paint runny. Apply the first color by spattering the paint evenly over the plate with a large paintbrush. You can add more thinner at this stage if you need to.

2 Allow the first color to dry before you apply the second
color, spattering it evenly over the surface. Allow to dry.

3 Spatter on the remaining colors, allowing the paint to dry
between coats. Once you are satisfied with the result, allow
the final coat to dry and bake the plate in the oven following
the manufacturer's instructions.

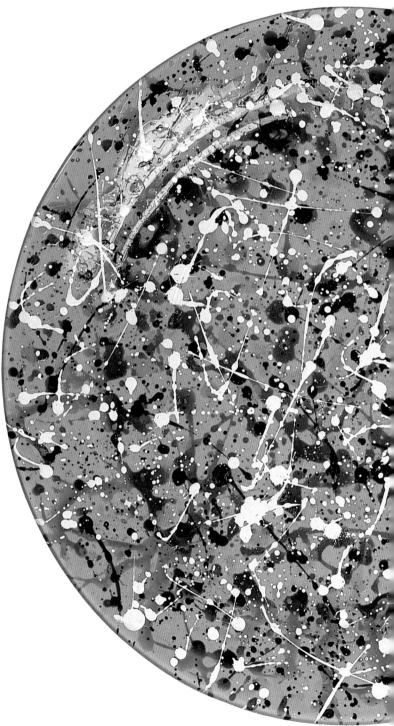

Country-Style Egg Cup

Using colored china means that you don't have to paint a background and can spend more time on the main design. The inspiration for this project came from some photographs of chickens that I had taken years before and had kept in a scrapbook, knowing that one day they would come in handy! Transferring a design to a curved surface is a little trickier than working on a flat surface, but it is worth the extra effort. You will find a template for the design at the back of the book.

MATERIALS

Yellow egg cups
Template from page 135
Tracing paper
Scissors
Transfer (carbon) paper
Masking tape
Pencil
Fine black permanent marker pen
Craft knife

Black, orange, and green ceramic pens
Black ceramic outliner paste

1 Decide how many birds you want on the egg cup. Trace the template on tracing paper, then cut around the design as closely as possible. Cut a piece of transfer (carbon) paper the same size and fix both pieces of paper to the egg cup with a little masking tape. (Make sure that the treated side of the transfer [carbon] paper is against the egg cup.) Draw over the design with a pencil.

2 Carefully remove the pattern so as not to smudge the transfer (carbon) lines, then go over them with permanent black pen.

3 Carefully fill in the body and face of your chicken(s) with the black ceramic pen.

4 Use the green pen to color in the neck area, and orange to fill in the rest. Allow to dry.

5 Add feathers to the birds by scratching off some of the paint with a craft knife to allow the background color to show through. Make an eye by scratching off a tiny patch of black.

6 Add evenly spaced dots over the surrounding area with the black outliner paste. When dry, bake in the oven following the manufacturer's instructions.

Doily Plate

This extremely unusual design is perfect for afternoon tea. The method of using an existing object such as a paper doily to create a pattern cuts down on preparation time and creates a very pleasing result. I have chosen a vivid pink because it is so reminiscent of old-fashioned iced cakes. You could paint a set of plates different colors to match your favorite teatime treats!

MATERIALS

White ceramic plate
Doily
Double-sided tape
Masking tape
Palette
Stipple brush
Craft knife

Red and white ceramic paint
Gold ceramic outliner paste

54

1 Having first made sure that all the gaps in the design are clear, fix the center of the doily to the plate with tiny pieces of double-sided tape. Use a little masking tape to secure it at the edges. (If the doily has a metallic side, place this against the plate, as it is less likely to stick to the surface than the paper side.)

2 Mix the red and white paint together on a palette to make a bright pink. Apply the mixture to the plate, using a stipple brush to work it into all the gaps in the doily. Repeat until you have a good depth of color, allowing the paint to dry between coats. (Don't forget to paint the areas of the plate that are covered by tape.)

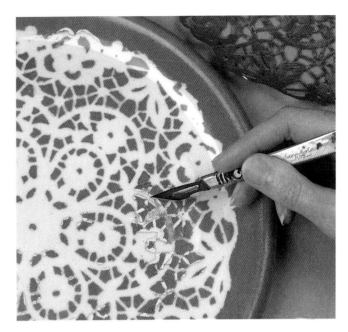

3 Once the paint is completely dry, peel off the doily to reveal the pattern underneath. Use a craft knife to help remove the doily.

4 If scraps of paper have become attached to the plate with the paint, carefully scratch them off with the knife.

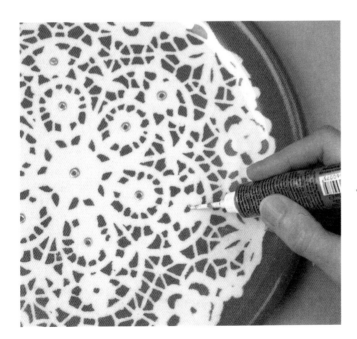

5 Add the gold detail to the plate using gold outliner paste. When dry, bake in the oven following the manufacturer's instructions.

Swirl Cup and Saucer

Inspiration for your own designs can come from a range of sources. The idea for this coffee set came from a book on 1950s-style interiors. Although the end result is quite sophisticated, the techniques used are the simple ones of masking and sponging. The gold swirl is drawn freehand.

MATERIALS

White ceramic cup and saucer
Ruler
Pencil
Masking film
Craft knife
Cutting mat
Tissue
Palette
Sponges
Paintbrush
Cotton swabs (buds)

Terracotta and dark green
    ceramic paints
Gold ceramic outliner paste

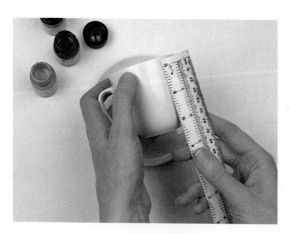

1 Use a ruler to gauge how large an area to decorate, and start to think about the colors you would like to use.

2 Draw the designs on masking film, then cut them out using a craft knife. On a cup this size, two large shapes work well.

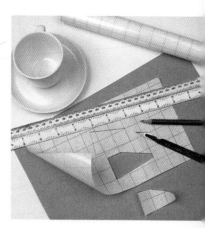

3 Position the masking film on the cup and peel off the backing paper. Use a tissue to smooth out any bubbles caught under the plastic, working from the center of the shape. (If the film is wrinkled at the edges, paint will seep under it.)

4 Place a little terracotta paint on the palette. Dip a sponge into the paint, then dab over any bare areas with the brush. Sponge color over the saucer (leaving the indentation in the center bare), then sponge color all over the cup.

5 When the paint is tacky but not fully dry, carefully peel off the mask. (Use the craft knife to lift a corner of the plastic so that you can get hold of it.) If any paint has seeped under the mask, clean it off with a damp cotton swab (bud).

6 When the paint is dry, sponge on a square of dark green. When the second color is dry, apply a swirl of gold outliner paste. Allow to dry, then bake in the oven following the manufacturer's instructions.

Tartan Picnic Set

This tea set came from a junk shop, where its good condition and lovely gold border caught my eye. Finding inexpensive china second hand means that you can paint it and use it for occasions such as picnics and parties where you might normally use plastic cups and plates. You can be less anxious about it getting broken and it looks so much nicer, too. It doesn't matter if your cups are a slightly different shape; simply adapt the Scottie design to suit the shape you're working with. The plates and saucers are open to interpretation, too. Remember, though, that the cups should be painted in the same colors.

Plates and saucers

MATERIALS

White ceramic plates and saucers
Masking tape
Stipple brush
Low-tack tape
Chisel brush
Steel ruler

Red, green, and black ceramic paint
Black ceramic pen

1 Form a grid pattern on the plate by applying two strips of masking tape horizontally and two strips vertically. Position the tape by eye or measure the plate first with a ruler if you want a more precise design. Stipple on one layer of red paint and allow it to dry.

2 When the masking tape has been removed you will be left with four broad white stripes. Apply low-tack tape along the left-hand side of two of these stripes to create narrow lines. Using a chisel brush and green paint, work your way along the lines, holding the brush at a diagonal angle. The aim is to make marks that represent the weave of a cloth. Allow to dry and remove the tape.

3 Repeat step 2 to form two more lines that run at right angles to the first two.

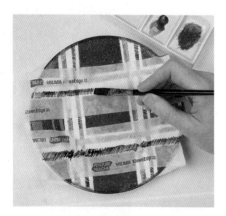

4 Repeat steps 2 and 3 with the black paint to create a pattern along the right-hand side of the stripes. Allow to dry and remove the tape.

5 To finish, draw a thin black line down the central, red area of the plate with the black ceramic pen. Draw a second line at right angles to the first to form a cross. When dry, bake in the oven following the manufacturer's instructions.

Cups

MATERIALS

White ceramic cups
Template from page 133
Tracing paper
Scissors
Transfer (carbon) paper
Masking tape
Pencil
Medium paintbrush

Black, green, red, and white
   ceramic paint

1 Decide how many dogs you will fit around your cup, then photocopy the Scottie template to size. (I used three on each of my cups.) Trace the template on tracing paper, then cut around the design as closely as possible. Cut a piece of transfer (carbon) paper to about the same size, then fix both the traced template and the transfer paper to the cup with a little masking tape, making sure that the transfer paper's treated side is against the cup. Draw over the design with a pencil.

2 Fill in the Scotties with the black paint using a medium paintbrush, leaving the nose and collar areas bare. Allow to dry.

5 Paint a thin black stripe around the bottom edge of each cup and allow to dry. Mix up a small amount of pink paint on the palette and paint in the noses. When dry, bake in the oven following the manufacturer's instructions.

3 Paint grass around the base of the cup with green paint using single, upward strokes. Allow to dry.

4 Use the red paint for the dog collar and add a stripe to the bottom edge of the cup with a fine brush. Let dry.

Blue and Gold Dish

Using masking tape cut with pinking shears is a simple and effective way to decorate a plain object. The effect of the pinking shears is to create a very refined line, and this technique can be applied to create bold, multicolored stripes on all kinds of flat and spherical surfaces. Here, I have combined blue and gold stripes for a classic effect, though you might like to add dots and squiggles to the pattern.

MATERIALS

White ceramic dish
Pinking shears
Masking tape

Blue ceramic paint
Blue and gold ceramic outliner paste

1 Cut strips of masking tape with pinking shears. Apply the strips to the dish vertically, leaving roughly equal spaces between them.

2 Sponge blue paint on the areas between the masking tape.

3 When the paint is completely dry, carefully peel off the masking tape.

4 Draw vertical lines down the center of the white, unpainted areas with blue outliner paste. Allow to dry. Paint gold lines over the blue bands in the same manner. When dry, bake in the oven following the manufacturer's instructions.

Aquatic
Toothbrush Holder

The watery effect that is achieved by stippling diluted paint on to a ceramic base makes it perfect for the bathroom. Glass paint is used over the silver outliner paste, as it is more transparent than ceramic paint. If you are feeling ambitious, you could transfer the design to wall tiles, providing that you prime the tiles beforehand, then varnish them when you have finished to protect all your hard work.

MATERIALS

White ceramic toothbrush holder
Stipple brush
Templates from page 132
Ceramic paint thinner
Tracing paper
Scissors
Transfer (carbon) paper
Masking tape
Pencil
Medium paintbrush
Sponge

Blue ceramic paint
Silver ceramic outliner paste
Green and white glass paint
Iridescent varnish (optional)

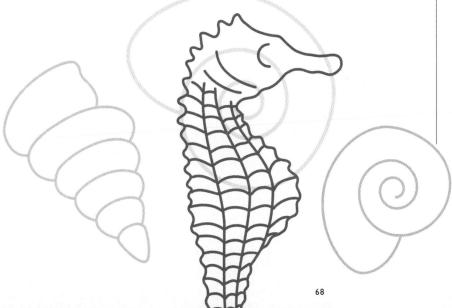

1 To help achieve the watery effect, dilute the blue paint with a little ceramic paint thinner. (Do not use water, as it will affect the paint's adhesion.) Quickly stipple the paint over the entire holder. Working rapidly will help produce the air bubbles that enhance the watery look of the paint. Allow to dry.

2 Photocopy the seahorse and shell templates to fit the size of the holder. Transfer the templates to tracing paper, then cut around the designs as closely as possible. Cut a piece of transfer (carbon) paper the same size and fix both pieces of paper to the holder with a little masking tape. (Make sure that the treated side is against the holder.) Draw over each design with a pencil.

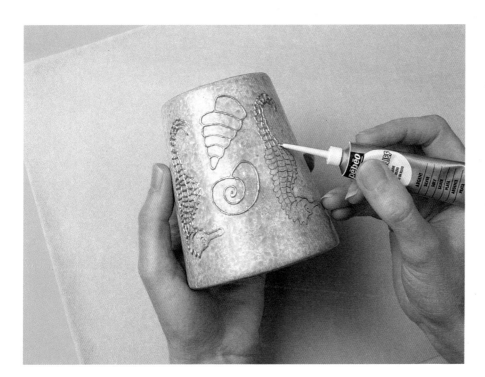

3 Remove the transfer (carbon) paper and template, then go over the transfer lines with silver outliner paste. Allow to dry.

4 Paint the seahorses with green glass paint using a medium paintbrush.

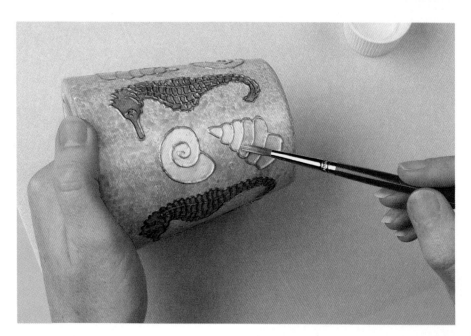

5 Once the seahorses have dried, fill in the shells with white glass paint. Allow to dry thoroughly.

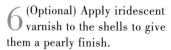

6 (Optional) Apply iridescent varnish to the shells to give them a pearly finish.

7 As a finishing touch, sponge some green glass paint around the rim of the holder. When dry, bake in the oven following the manufacturer's instructions.

Opposite Create a starfish soap dish to complement your aquatic toothbrush holder. The starfish is outlined in silver, then painted over in orange ceramic paint.

Counting Sheep Cup and Saucer

Could this be a new cure for insomnia? Once you've drunk your hot chocolate from this enormous cup and saucer and counted to a hundred, you'll be asleep in no time. If you can bear to part with it, this set would make an ideal gift. You can also personalize it by adding a name to the cup with gold outliner.

MATERIALS

White ceramic cup and saucer
Large, medium and fine paintbrushes
Scissors
Masking film
Sponge

Green, blue, white, and black ceramic paint
Gold ceramic outliner paste

1 With the large paintbrush, paint the grassy area at the base of the cup with broad, horizontal strokes. While the cup is drying, mask off the indentation in the center of the saucer with a circle of masking film. Paint broad strokes of green paint from the center of the saucer to the edge of the rim. Allow to dry.

2 Clean the brush, then paint the sky with broad strokes of blue paint. Allow to dry.

3 Create the body of each sheep by sponging white paint into rough ovals where the grass and sky meet. (I had three sheep on my cup.) Allow to dry.

4 Mix up a little gray paint, then use the medium brush to paint the heads, ears, legs, and feet of each sheep. Use a fine brush to add swirls to the wool. Allow to dry.

5 Add detail to the feet and each face in black with the fine brush. Allow to dry.

6 Write the numbers with the gold outliner pen. When dry, bake in the oven following the manufacturer's instructions.

Harlequin Plates

This striking design was inspired

by the diamond-patterned

costume worn by traditional

harlequin characters. The gold

paint contrasts well with any

bright color, including plain

white. Because of its geometrical

nature, the design works

particularly well on square

surfaces.

MATERIALS

Square white ceramic plates
Gold permanent pen
Ruler

Gold and orange or turquoise
    ceramic paint
Gold ceramic outliner paste

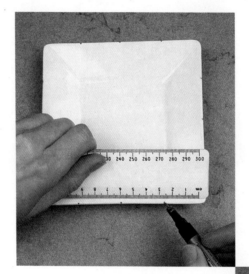

1 Find the center point on the outer edge of each side of the plate, then mark it with a permanent gold pen. Measure the distance between these points and the corners of the plate and mark the halfway point. There will now be three marks on each side.

2 Measure the center points on the inside of the plate and mark them, then mark the four inner corners.

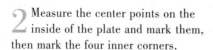

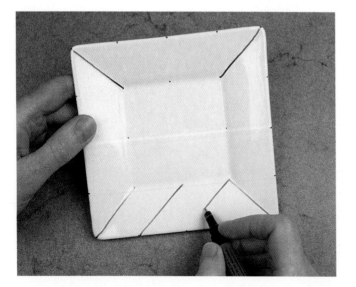

4 Draw diagonal lines between the marks in the opposite
direction to form a crisscross pattern.

3 Use the gold pen to join the inner and outer marks. This
will give you a series of diagonal lines across the rim.

6 If desired, fill in the rest of the pattern with orange or turquoise ceramic paint. Allow to dry. Mark each point of the pattern with a dot of gold outliner paste. When dry, bake in the oven following the manufacturer's instructions.

5 Fill in half the pattern with gold ceramic paint. Allow to dry.

Leafy Pasta Dish

The leaf design on the border of this dish is made with a simple, linoleum stamp and some lines of contrasting color. Linoleum is a durable material, and stamps cut from it can be used time and again. Keep the carved shapes simple, as this makes them easier to cut out. Using small stamps like the leaf in this project is a little fiddly, but no other material will allow you to create the same amount of detail.

MATERIALS

White ceramic pasta dish
Linoleum
Permanent marker pen
Linoleum-cutting tool
Craft knife
Cutting mat
Medium paintbrush

Green ceramic paint
Green and orange ceramic
    outliner paste

1 Draw the outline and veins of a leaf on a piece of linoleum with a pen, then gouge out the design with the linoleum-cutting tool. Take care to cut away from you.

2 Carefully cut around the edge of the stamp with a sharp craft knife.

3 Use the brush to apply green ceramic paint to the engraved surface of the stamp, then press the stamp firmly on to the rim of the plate. Stamp a leaf at quarter points around the dish, then stamp another leaf between each of these.

4 Stamp either side of each leaf so that you have eight sprigs of three leaves equally spaced around the rim.

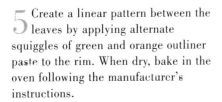

5 Create a linear pattern between the leaves by applying alternate squiggles of green and orange outliner paste to the rim. When dry, bake in the oven following the manufacturer's instructions.

Painting Glassware

THE MATERIALS USED IN CERAMIC PAINTING CAN BE APPLIED JUST AS SUCCESSFULLY TO FROSTED AND CLEAR GLASS OBJECTS. IN THIS SECTION, MASKING WITH FLUID AND GILDING ARE ADDED TO THE BASIC CERAMIC-PAINTING TECHNIQUES COVERED IN THE PREVIOUS CHAPTER.

MATERIALS

Frosted glass plate
Ruler
Masking tape
Pencil
Sponge
Medium paintbrush
While tile

Blue and green ceramic paint
Silver ceramic outliner paste

Frosted Glass Plate

Frosted glass makes an ideal base

for a simple design. Here, lines

of silver outliner paste are

combined with stamped shapes in

blue and green to striking effect.

I have used ceramic paint for

this project, because its opacity

works well with that of the glass.

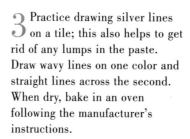

1 Measure the circumference of the plate following the instructions given on page 12. Divide the area of the plate into eight sections, marking each section with pencil.

2 Cut a piece of sponge for each of the two colors, making them small enough to fit within the sections marked on the plate. Stamp the first color in four quarters of the plate. Stamp the remaining four areas with the second color. Allow to dry.

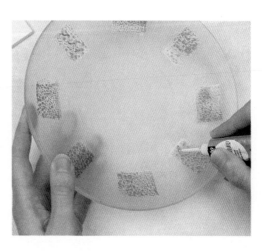

3 Practice drawing silver lines on a tile; this also helps to get rid of any lumps in the paste. Draw wavy lines on one color and straight lines across the second. When dry, bake in an oven following the manufacturer's instructions.

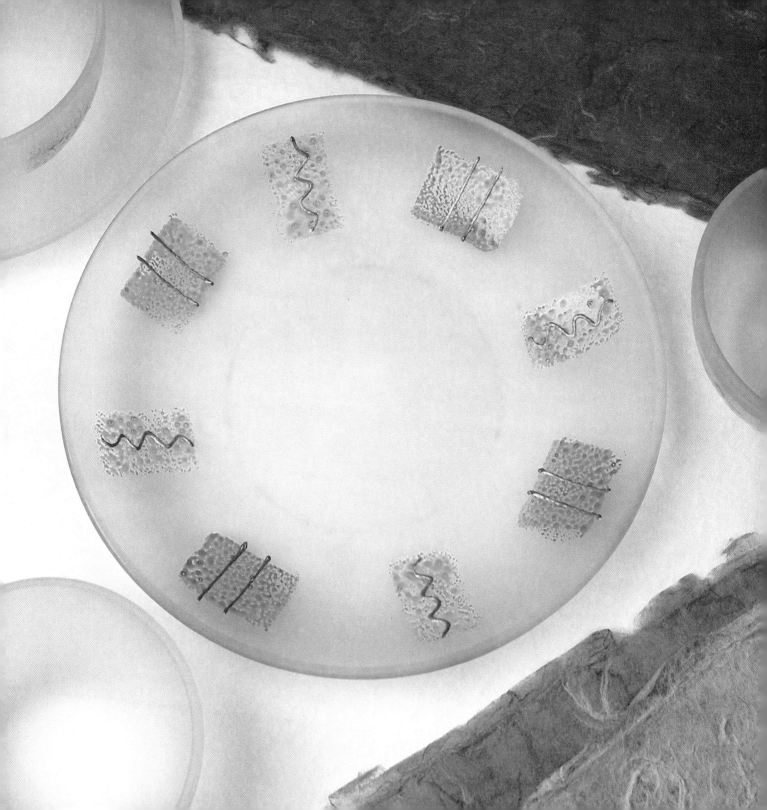

Striped Spaghetti Jar

This technique produces a very different effect to the one you would achieve if you painted the stripes on the outside of the jar with a brush. Allowing the paint to drip of its own accord gives the lines a nice uneven edge. The length of the paintbrush will determine how much of the jar you can decorate. I have chosen two contrasting colors, but multicolored stripes would work just as well.

1 Begin the first line as far down the jar as the length of your brush will allow you to reach. Drip red glass paint on the inside of the jar in the same spot until it starts to run. Keep the jar rolling so that the drip travels around the jar until it meets the point where it began. The paint will tend to spread if the jar is left in one position, so roll it from time to time to keep the paint moving until it is completely dry.

2 Repeat at regular intervals along the jar, leaving a gap between each line. Allow each line to dry before painting the next.

3 Repeat the process using the green paint, placing these lines between the red ones. When dry, bake in the oven following the manufacturer's instructions.

MATERIALS

Clear glass storage
    jar with lid
Fine paintbrush
Clear varnish
    (optional)

Red and green glass
    paint

4 Paint the sides of the lid with one or both of the glass paints so that it matches the jar. Allow to dry. (If the lid is metallic, it won't be suitable for baking. To protect it from scratches, you may wish to apply a coat of clear varnish.)

Sunburst
Tealight
Holders

I chose square-sided jars for this project because they make the task of positioning the suns very simple. If you have cylindrical jars, place the sun templates at regular intervals around them. Work on one color at a time, allowing each to dry before applying the next. However, when applying the gel in step 5, cover all four sides at the same time, then let each jar stand on its base to dry. This can take quite a long time, depending on how thickly the gel is applied.

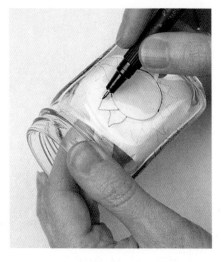

MATERIALS

Square-sided glass jar
Template from page 134
Scissors
Masking tape
Fine black permanent marker pen
Medium and fine paintbrushes

Yellow, red, and orange glass paint
Black glass outliner paste
Blue crystal gel with a fine nozzle

1 Photocopy four sun templates to fit the size of the jar. Cut them out and stick them to the inside of the jar with tape. Trace over each sun shape with the black pen, then remove the paper templates. Continue the rays out to the edges of the other suns so that they join up.

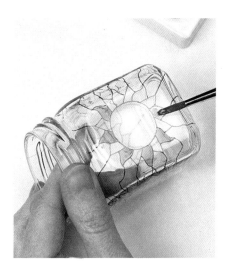

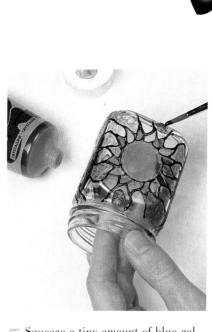

2 Paint alternate rays on each of the four suns with the yellow paint. Allow to dry.

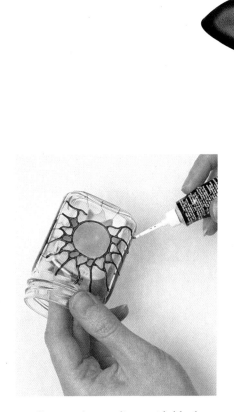

4 Go over the pen lines with black outliner paste. Do one side at a time and allow each to dry before working on the next.

3 Working on one side of the jar at a time, paint the remaining rays red. Allow to dry, then fill in the suns with orange. Make sure the suns are dry before proceeding to the next step.

5 Squeeze a tiny amount of blue gel on to alternate areas surrounding the suns and work the gel to an even consistency with a brush to create a dappled effect. Allow to dry completely, then bake in the oven following the manufacturer's instructions.

Cactus Margarita Glasses

Every cocktail should have its own glass, and the inverted sombrero is the classic one for a Margarita. If you prefer to stick to lemonade, these glasses will bring a touch of Mexican sunshine to that, too. This design can also be adapted to decorate a set of clear glass dessert plates or straight-sided glasses.

MATERIALS

Cocktail glasses
Acetate
Template from page 134
Scissors
Masking tape
Medium paintbrush

Green and yellow glass paint
Green and yellow glass outliner paste

1 Planning the design is all part of the fun! Experiment with different colors and techniques on a sheet of acetate before you begin to paint the Margarita glasses.

2 Photocopy the cactus template to fit the size of your glass and decide how many you will need. Cut out the shapes as neatly as possible and secure them to the inside of the glass with tape, design facing out, ensuring that you leave an even amount of space between them.

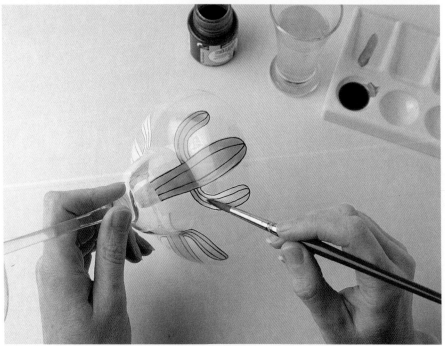

3 Fill in each cactus shape with green glass paint, taking care to stay within the lines. Allow to dry.

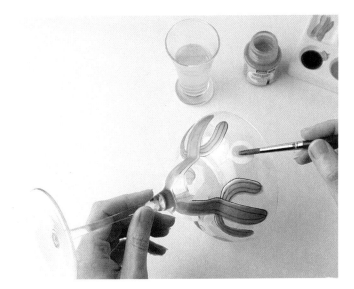

4 Cut out enough identically sized paper circles to fit between the cacti, then attach them to the inside of the glass with masking tape. Paint over the shapes with yellow glass paint. Allow to dry.

5 Draw in the needles on the cacti with green outliner paste, following the lines on the template. Allow to dry.

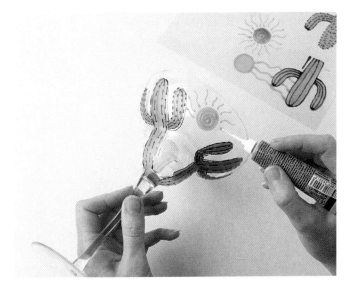

6 Add detail to the center of each sun and draw rays around them using yellow outliner paste. When dry, remove the templates. Bake the glasses in the oven following the manufacturer's instructions.

Mondrian-Style Picture Frame

This simple project, which uses the techniques of masking and stippling, was inspired by the work of Piet Mondrian, a Dutch abstract artist. The rectangular design can easily be adapted to fit a square, and the clean lines provide a neat border for a favorite photograph or print. To set off my frame, I painted a colorful image reminiscent of the work of the Spanish painter, Joan Miró.

MATERIALS

Clip frame
Sheet of paper
Fine black permanent
   marker pen
Scissors
Low-tack masking tape
Steel ruler

Sponges
Craft knife

White, red, yellow, and
   blue ceramic paint
Black glass outliner paste

1 Create a template by tracing around the glass on a piece of paper. Remove the glass, then draw a broad margin down three sides of the paper, adding the other divisions using the photograph opposite as a guide. Place the glass over the template and transfer the design to it using a ruler and the black marker pen.

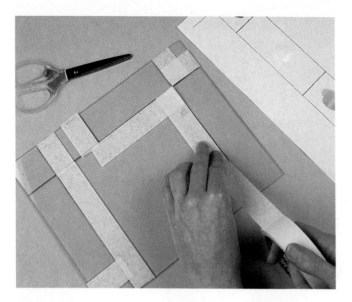

2 Use low-tack tape to mask off the areas that won't be painted white. (You might find it helpful to mark each area of the pattern with a dab of its intended color.)

3 Apply white paint with a sponge until the surface is covered evenly. Apply additional coats until the paint is completely opaque, letting each coat dry between applications.

4 When the white areas are completely dry, remove the masking tape. Apply fresh strips around the areas that you intend to paint red, yellow, and blue. Sponge on several coats of each color, letting each coat dry before applying the next.

5 With the craft knife, carefully remove the tape. (If any of the white paint lifts off when the tape is removed, simply dab on a little fresh paint with the sponge.)

6 Go over the black pen lines that separate the colors with the black outliner. When dry, bake in the oven following the manufacturer's instructions.

Squiggly Shot Glasses

The simple pattern used in this project works especially well when painted on a group of items. A set of six multicolored glasses, such as the one shown here, would make a lovely gift. The trick to making the best of this design is to choose colors that work well together, and it's worth testing a few combinations on an old jar or a piece of acetate before you begin. I have used complementary colors on some of the glasses, and matching colors on others. Try to make lines in one sweep and keep the outliner pen moving to reduce the chances of making a nasty blob. If this does happen, you can always wipe the paint off before it dries.

MATERIALS

Shot glasses
Medium chisel brush

Glass paint and glass outliner paste
   in assorted colors

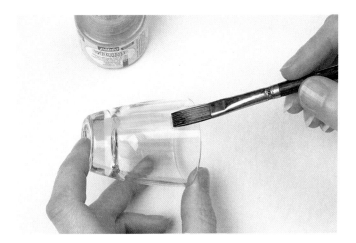

1 Using a chisel brush, paint a stripe of glass paint from the base of the glass to the top. Repeat until you have four vertical stripes at equal distance from each other. Allow to dry.

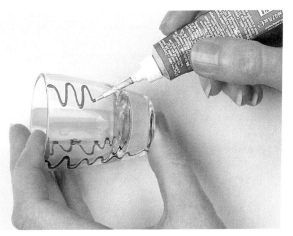

2 Draw a wavy line between each stripe, working from top to bottom of the glass. Here, turquoise outliner paste was used to contrast with the yellow. Allow to dry.

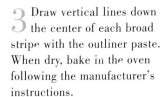

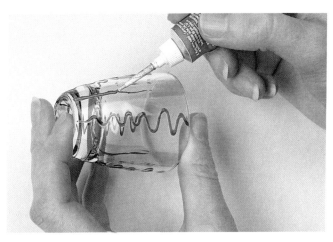

3 Draw vertical lines down the center of each broad stripe with the outliner paste. When dry, bake in the oven following the manufacturer's instructions.

Gilded Goldfish Bowl

This project is for people who like the idea of keeping fish, but who don't want the responsibility that that entails. If you already have a goldfish, you could put him in your finished bowl to give him some company. To minimize the risk of damaging the gold and silver leaf, I recommend that you carefully wash the bowl by hand rather than in the dishwasher. If you intend to use the bowl purely for decoration, you might want to consider scattering a few pebbles on the bottom and adding water tinted with a little blue food coloring to contrast with the orange of the painted fish.

MATERIALS

Large glass bowl
Gold pen
Acrylic size
Medium and fine paintbrushes
Gold and silver leaf
Cotton balls (optional)
Craft knife
Template from page 134
Scissors
Masking tape
Tracing paper
Transfer (carbon) paper
Pencil
Burnisher or dried-up ballpoint pen

Green, yellow, orange, black, and
 white glass paint
Iridescent crystal gel with a fine nozzle

1 Turn the bowl upside down and draw fronds of seaweed all around the base and up the sides of the bowl with a gold pen, keeping the shapes of the leaves to a simple pattern. Apply the acrylic size to two or three fronds at a time and let it dry for a few minutes until it becomes "tacky." When the size is ready, hold a sheet of gold leaf over it and press down gently using a finger or cotton ball. Rub the gold leaf into the size, then wipe away the excess leaf and neaten the edges with a craft knife. Repeat until all the seaweed is covered. (Always follow the manufacturer's instructions when using metal leaf, as the methods of applying the product can vary.)

2 Turn the bowl the right side up. Photocopy the goldfish template and cut out as many as will fit comfortably above the fronds of seaweed. Attach the paper fish to the inside of the bowl facing out.

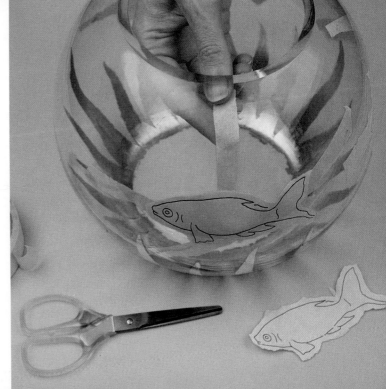

3 Apply acrylic size over one of the fish shapes with a fine brush, taking care to stay within the lines of the template. Allow the size to become tacky.

4 Press the silver leaf over the fish shape with a finger or cotton ball. Rub away any excess and clean up uneven lines with a craft knife. Repeat steps 3 and 4 with as many fish as you have, then remove the templates from inside the bowl.

5 Make a tracing of the fish template, complete with scales and other details, and cut out a piece of transfer (carbon) paper to roughly the same size and shape. Attach the paper, treated side down, to the silver fish with a little tape. Draw over the tracing paper with a pencil to transfer the detail to the silver leaf. Remove the tracing to reveal the transfer lines. Repeat with as many fish as you have.

6 Use the burnisher or dried-up ballpoint pen to etch the transfer lines into each gilded fish.

7 Turn the bowl upside down. Apply green glass paint to the seaweed with a medium brush. Start at the base of the bowl and paint toward the tips of the fronds, which should be left gold to catch the light and to give the bowl depth. Allow to dry.

8 Etch lines into the fronds with the burnisher or ball-point pen. When you have finished, turn the bowl the right side up again.

9 Paint the goldfish. Start by applying yellow with a fine paintbrush along the top and bottom edge. While this is still wet, apply orange on top of this and behind the gills. Using a fine paintbrush, draw lines of orange in the fins and tail and go over some of the scales. (Be sure to leave a few bare patches of silver leaf as a contrast to the paint.)

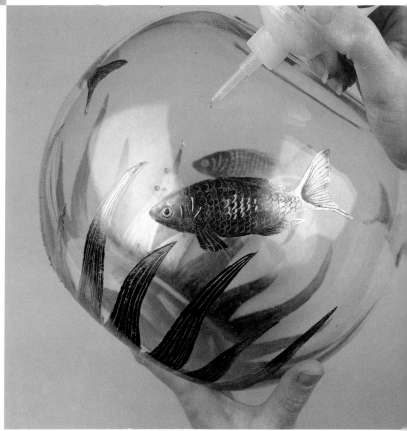

10 Complete each fish by outlining some of the scales with black and white paint, and paint the eye. Finally, add tiny air bubbles above each fish with dots of iridescent gel.

Mediterranean Carafe

The use of rich colors like burgundy and gold can transform a simple glass carafe into something classic and elegant. The grapes design can also be reduced on a photocopier and transferred to wine glasses. The use of gold ceramic paint under the glass paint gives the grapes a luminescent quality that can't be achieved with glass paint alone. For a more opaque finish, sponge gold paint over the whole carafe before transferring the design.

MATERIALS

Glass carafe
Template from page 135
Transfer (carbon) paper
Masking tape
Pencil
Medium and fine paintbrushes

Gold ceramic paint
Purple, two shades of green, and
    white glass paint
Gold glass outliner paste

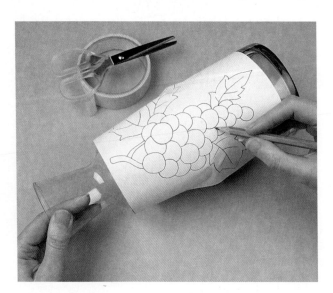

1 Photocopy the bunch of grapes template to the correct size. Cut a piece of transfer (carbon) paper to the same size and tape it to the carafe, treated side down. Draw over the template with a pencil to transfer the design to the carafe.

2 Using a medium paintbrush, paint over the entire design with gold ceramic paint, making sure that the pencil line remains clear around the fruit and the leaves. Allow to dry.

3 Paint over the grapes with the purple paint. Make even, vertical brushstrokes that follow the shape of each grape. Allow to dry.

4 Darken the right-hand side of each grape by adding several more strokes of purple. This will help to define the shape of the fruit. Allow to dry.

5 Give the leaves some depth by painting them with the two shades of green paint. Begin with the lighter green and add random patches of darker paint while the lighter is still wet so that they merge a little. Let dry, then add veins to the leaves with the darker paint using the fine brush. Allow to dry.

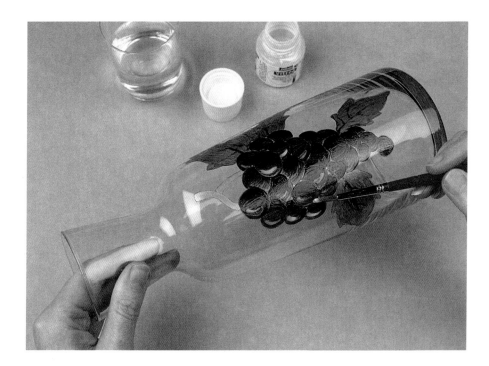

6 Paint highlights on the upper left-hand part of each grape with white paint and a fine brush. Allow to dry.

7 Finally, add curly tendrils to the bunch of grapes with gold outliner paste. When dry, bake in the oven following the manufacturer's instructions.

Copper Scroll Vase

In this project, a few daubs of color and some bold lines are used to transform a plain glass vase into something unique. Applying the paint with a paper towel instead of a sponge creates a lovely, broken effect. The copper lines that are painted on the vase at the end of the project catch the light in a particularly eye-catching way. Here, ceramic paints are used because their opacity is so well suited to the frosted background.

MATERIALS

Frosted glass vase
Paper towels
Fine paintbrush
White tile (optional)

Orange, yellow, and copper
ceramic paint

1 With a dry paper towel, dab orange paint randomly over the surface of the vase.

2 Repeat with the yellow paint. Add further daubs of orange until you are happy with the effect. Allow to dry.

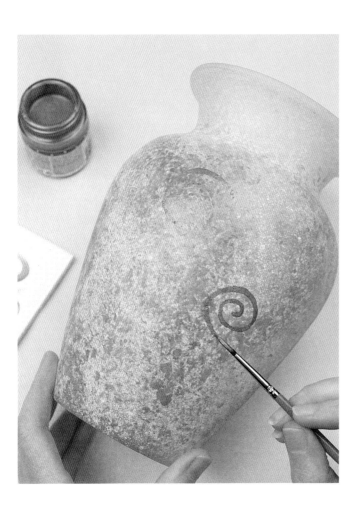

3 Use the fine paintbrush to apply swirls and squiggles of copper paint all over the vase. (You might like to practice painting lines on a tile first.) When dry, bake in an oven following the manufacturer's instructions.

Daisy Vase

Attaching brightly colored glass nuggets to a plain vase is a really easy way to transform what could be a rather ordinary container into something unique. For this project, white flowers are used to accentuate the different colors of the nuggets. I have used ceramic paint for this project because it is more opaque than glass paint, thus ensuring that the flowers and leaves really stand out.

MATERIALS

Glass vase
Templates from page 135
Masking film
Craft knife
Cutting mat
Stipple brush
Stencil board
Low-tack masking tape
Flat-backed glass nuggets
Strong glass glue (superglue)

White and green ceramic paint

1 Decide how many copies of the daisy template you will need to cover the vase, then trace them on to masking film. Cut out the daisy shapes and discard them. (Alternatively, you might like to keep them for another project.) Stick the flower shapes evenly over the vase, pressing the masking film down firmly to get rid of any trapped air that might cause wrinkles.

2 Apply white ceramic paint to the daisies with a stipple brush and allow to dry. Repeat until you achieve an even coverage, allowing the paint to dry between applications.

3 Carefully peel off the masking film. (You may find it helpful to use a craft knife to lift the film off the glass.)

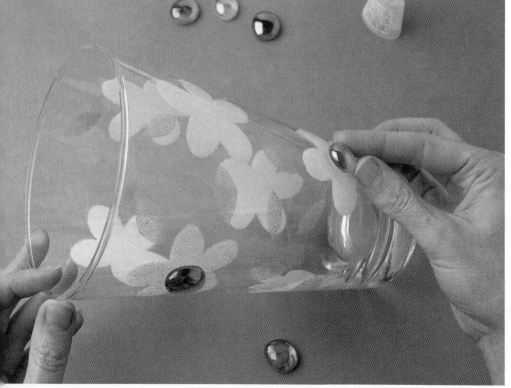

4 Cut two leaf-shaped stencils of different sizes from stencil board. Stipple green paint over the larger stencil, holding it in place with low-tack tape. Move it around the vase until you have enough large leaves. Repeat with the smaller stencil, filling in the areas between the larger leaves and the daisies. When the paint is completely dry, bake the vase in the oven following the manufacturer's instructions.

5 Adhere a glass nugget to the center of each daisy with strong glass glue.

Confetti Cocktail Glasses

The idea behind this project was to create a design that subtly brought the glass to life with bright, contrasting colors. The benefit of using the new transparent outliner pastes is that you can wash the glasses in the dishwasher, providing that the glasses themselves can withstand it. The simple shape of this cocktail glass provides a good base for a colorful spiral pattern. Choose colors that match well, and you can't go wrong. If you find the spiral design a bit tricky, try covering the glass in multicolored circles or dots instead.

MATERIALS

Clear glasses

Turquoise, yellow, and orange
glass outliner paste

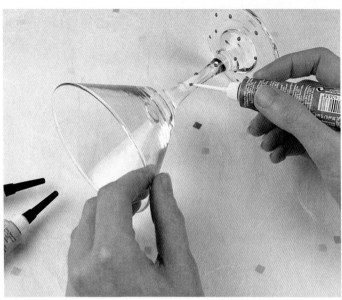

2 Holding the glass by its base, add the other colors in the same way. Here I have matched one cool color – turquoise – with two warmer ones. Allow to dry.

1 Paint dots of your first color all over the stem and base of the glass, making sure that they are evenly spaced. Allow the dots to dry completely.

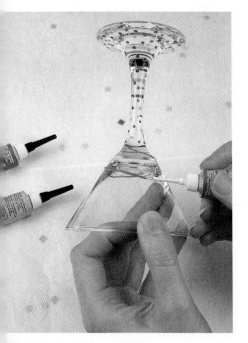

3 Turn the glass over and support the rim on the work surface. Begin to draw a wide spiral with the outliner paste around the glass with your first color by starting at the top of the stem and slowly turning the glass. Try to keep the paste moving so that the line is steady. Allow to dry.

4 Once the first spiral is complete, it is easier to draw the others. Follow the line of the first color with your second and allow it to dry. Repeat with the final color and allow to dry. Bake in the oven following the manufacturer's instructions.

Marbled Perfume Bottle

To achieve the best results with this technique, it is important to work quickly, and to have all the materials close at hand. I have chosen a bottle that has lots of different "segments," but a straight-sided one would look just as nice. I worked on a segment at a time, to take full advantage of the effect of the thinner. (Once the paint begins to dry, it doesn't run as well.) You may introduce as many colors to the design as you like, or color each area differently. The outcome is fairly random, but you might like to experiment first on a piece of acetate or an old jar to get an idea of how the finished piece will look.

MATERIALS

Glass bottle
Palette
A paintbrush for each color plus
    one for the thinner
Glass paint thinner

Blue and white glass paint

1 Mix some blue glass paint with some thinner to dilute the paint and make it more transparent. The ratio should be about half and half.

2 The way you do this step will depend on the shape of your bottle. The segments on this particular bottle meant that I could apply paint to one section at a time. (A square-sided container would enable you to do the same.) Apply the diluted paint to the first section.

3 Add dots of white paint to the area you have just painted, then dots of undiluted blue. This will help create some depth of color.

4 Add dots of pure thinner to help the spreading process. Repeat on each section until the entire bottle is covered. When dry, bake in the oven following the manufacturer's instructions.

Spiral Sundae Dish

MATERIALS

Sundae glass
China marker
Masking fluid
Fine paintbrush
Sponge

Red glass paint

Spirals are always a popular motif, and are easy to draw freehand. I have drawn the spirals first with a china marker, then followed the lines with the masking fluid. The advantage of drawing the design out first with a china marker, is that it can be rubbed off and redrawn if you are not happy with the effect. This technique can also be applied to a vase: the light from a sunny windowsill subtly enhances the effect of the colors.

1 Draw spirals on the outside of the sundae dish with a china marker, then paint over them with masking fluid. Let dry.

2 Apply a thin coat of red glass paint over the spirals with a piece of sponge, then allow to dry.

3 Peel off the masking-fluid spirals, then bake the dish in the oven following the manufacturer's instructions

Templates

Instructions on how to use the templates can be found on page 15.

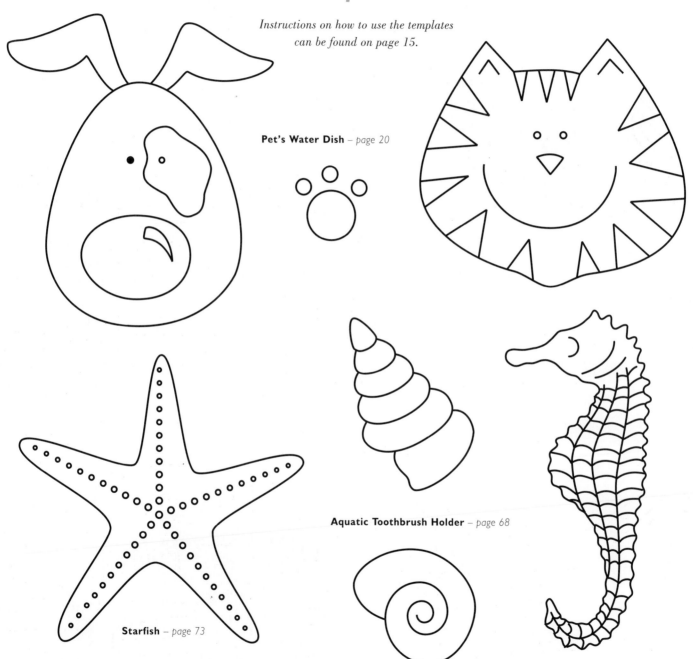

Pet's Water Dish – *page 20*

Starfish – *page 73*

Aquatic Toothbrush Holder – *page 68*

*(See page 41 for
Turtle head templates.)*

Tartan Picnic Set – *page 64*

Turtle Serving Dish – *page 37*

1950s Plate (red) – *page 42*

Sunburst Tealight Holders – *page 93*

Gilded Goldfish Bowl – *page 106*

Cactus Margarita Glasses – *page 96*

1950s Plate (blue) – *page 42*

Country-Style Egg cup – *page 51*

Mediterranean Carafe – *page 112*

Daisy Vase – *page 121*

Sources

The following is a list of sources for the "cold" (air-dry) and thermo-set (oven-cured) glass and ceramic paints that are used in this book. These companies generally sell their products exclusively to retailers, but if you can't find a store in your area that carries a particular item or will accept a request for an order, they will gladly direct you to the retailer nearest you that carries their products and offer technical assistance.

DecoArt
Highways 150 and 27
Stanford, KY 40484
(606) 365-3193
http://www.decoart.com/
Ultra Gloss Acrylic Enamels

Deka
P.O. Box 309
Morrisville, VT 05661
(800) 232-3352
Deka-Transparent

Delta Technical Coatings
2550 Pellissier Place
Whittier, CA 90601-1505
(562) 695-7969
http://www.deltacrafts.com/
Ceramcoat Acrylic Paint,
Air-Dry PermEnamel Tile and
Glass Paint, Textured Gel,
and Transparent Glass Paints

Pebeo of America, Inc.
555 Vermont Route 78
P.O. Box 717
Swanton, VT 05488
(819) 829-5012
http://www.pebeo.com/
Ceramic, Cernes Reliefs
Outliners, Gel Crystal, Liquid
Crystal, Pebeo Deco, Porcelaine
150, Vitrail, Vitrea 160

Plaid Enterprises, Inc.
1649 International Court
Norcross, GA 30093
(678) 291-8100
http://www.plaidonline.com/
Apple Barrell Gloss Enamel

Acknowledgments

The publishers would like to thank John Wright at Pébéo UK Ltd for kindly supplying the paints used in this book.

All projects by Alma Caira, apart from pages 16, 58-60, 86, 88-9, 116-19.

Photography: Shona Wood
Templates: Duke Design
Design: Janet James
Project Manager: Janet Ravenscroft

Index

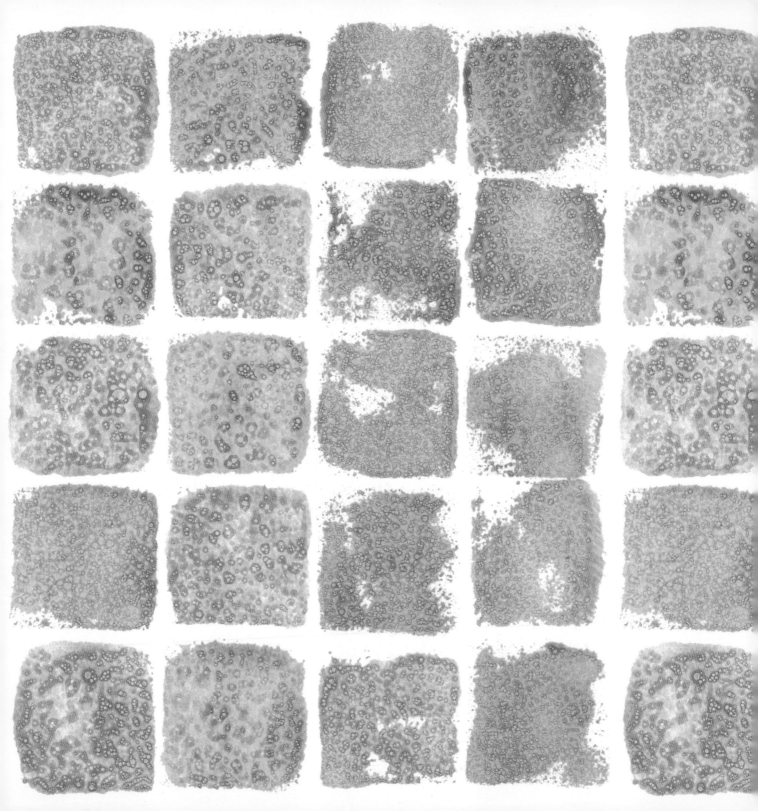

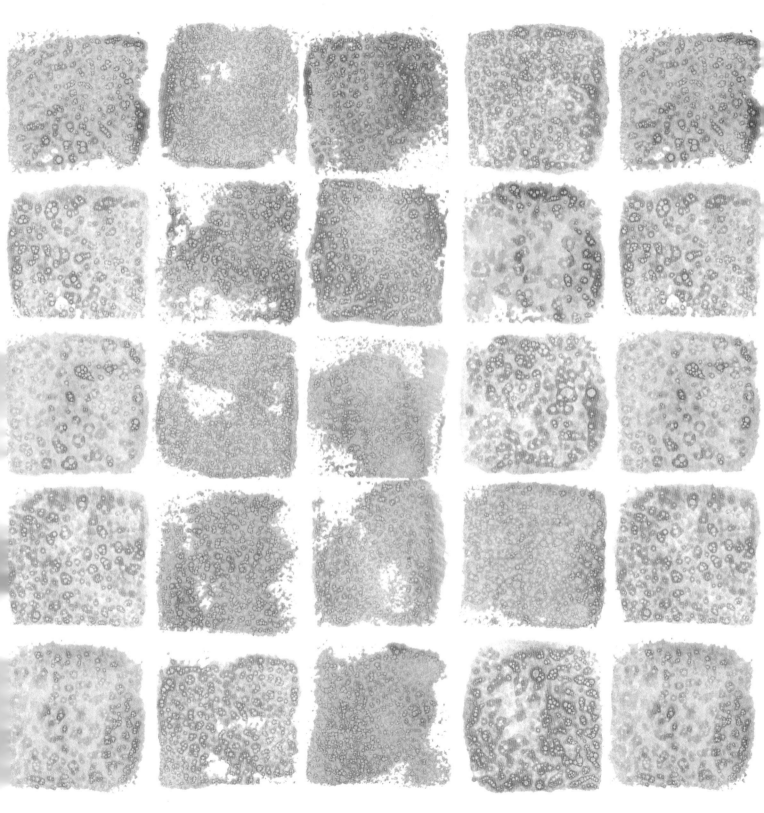